ADULTERY
The Snare of an Affair

JUNE HUNT

AspirePress

Torrance, California

Adultery: The Snare of an Affair
Copyright © 2013 Hope For The Heart
All rights reserved.
Aspire Press, a division of Rose Publishing, Inc.
4733 Torrance Blvd., #259
Torrance, California 90503 USA
www.aspirepress.com

Register your book at www.aspirepress.com/register
Get inspiration via email, sign up at www.aspirepress.com

Printed in the United States of America
010513DP

CONTENTS

ear friend,

How would you feel if your husband sent you out of state to your mother's home for a month? He had already shipped off three of your children to summer camp and the 17-year-old 1,000 miles away to a summer job.

Then you return home only to realize, "Someone's been eating my porridge!" You wish it were a child's fairy tale like *Goldilocks and The Three Bears* or just a bad dream, but this shock is reality. "Someone's been wearing my clothes, someone's been using my perfume, someone's been sleeping in my bed." This was all true. This happened to my mother.

Nothing is more devastating than adultery. Nothing wounds a woman's worth like infidelity. I know. I saw my mother's sense of value drop to rock bottom. I grew up in a home where betrayal knew no bounds.

My mother, who admitted making a series of wrong choices, became emotionally drawn to a man double her age. Ultimately, she married my dad. But it wasn't until my teenage years that I saw the devastation of adultery first hand.

Words are inadequate to express the anger, pain and anguish I carried deep within my soul as I discovered my father was having one affair after another, with woman after woman. I felt violated by my father's sexual involvements. I felt a strong sense of betrayal on behalf of our whole family. And I felt I was my mother's personal protector—yet as hard as I tried, I couldn't protect her.

As devastating as this experience was, I also saw my mother drawn into a deep dependence on the Lord. She took to heart the Scripture, *"Your Maker is your husband— the LORD Almighty is his name"* (Isaiah 54:5).

If you have been betrayed by your mate— or if you have been caught in the *snare of an affair*—I want you to know that in God there is hope for you and your situation. Although this is a difficult road, you are not traveling alone. The Lord says, *"I will instruct you and teach you in the way you should go; I will counsel you and watch over you"* (Psalm 32:8).

May God use the truths in this book to bring healing to your heart and hope to your soul.

Yours in the Lord's hope,

June Hunt

ADULTERY
The Snare of an Affair

Look at how that long, lingering stare subtly becomes the snare. But how could this happen to *him*? He is their fearless warrior—determined and disciplined. And he is their king—held in highest esteem.

Yet one fateful evening, when he should be overseeing his army, he becomes mesmerized at the sight of a beautiful woman, consumed with lust for this *married* woman. Although he, too, is married, he forsakes his wedding vows and behind closed doors commits adultery.

Somehow this one, solitary evening of selfish pleasure has just opened the door to other unthinkable sins. Indeed his own sexual compromise leads to unimaginable consequences.

Has your life been gripped by the agony of adultery? Has your life been forever changed by the snare of an affair? Since marriage was designed by God to be a lifelong covenant commitment, He will judge those who break the marriage covenant.

The Bible states clearly that ...

"Marriage should be honored by all, and the marriage bed kept pure, for God will judge the adulterer and all the sexually immoral."
(Hebrews 13:4)

DEFINITIONS

"But David remained in Jerusalem" (2 Samuel 11:1). These ominous words foreshadow far more than a king who fails to join his army. It's springtime. Weather conditions are favorable. Army provisions are ample. It's the customary time for kings to go to war. But not King David! Instead, he sends his commander while his troops wage war without him. Meanwhile, he stays home, walking the halls of his palace. This scenario is most unusual because David's history reveals he doesn't hold back from battle, but rather runs toward it.

As a young shepherd boy, when an entire army cowers, David accepts an impossible challenge: He comes against the arrogant Goliath and kills the Philistine giant. Soon he is leading King Saul's army into one victory after another. Then later as God's next anointed king, he bravely goes to battle to consolidate the kingdom. Yet now with his military battling many miles away, King David finds himself in an entirely different battle *and his defenses are dangerously down.*

Interestingly, those who walk through the door of adultery assume, *I won't get caught. No one will know. It's no big deal.* Oh, how blind they are. They simply do not see how their own selfish choices will reap severe results. The Bible even warns ...

> **"Do not be deceived: God cannot be mocked. A man reaps what he sows."**
> **(Galatians 6:7)**

WHAT IS Adultery?

The king has been restless this particular evening, walking aimlessly around the roof of his palace. From the corner of his eye David notices light casting a golden glow across a reclining silhouette.

He looks, and soon his eyes are locked in a lustful stare. He gazes upon this woman—a *"very beautiful"* woman (2 Samuel 11:2)— bathing by lamp light in her courtyard. Now he is transfixed and trouble is on the horizon.

As a man of God, David is familiar with all of God's commands, including the seventh of His Ten Commandments: God forbids adultery. God expressly forbids sexual relations with another person's mate.

But the king turns a blind eye to Scripture, so that he can scope out the enticing scene. Soon, his visual sin takes a strategic spin. First David sends someone to find out who the woman is, then he sends messengers to bring her to the palace.

He's a married man, and Bathsheba is married too, but her husband is far away—ironically, fighting in David's army.

So lust looms and blooms, which proves to be a pitfall. What happens next will forever change the course of David's life.

> **"She came to him,
> and he slept with her."**
> **(2 Samuel 11:4)**

▶ **Adultery** is voluntary sexual intercourse between a married person and another person who is not his or her lawful spouse.[1] Spiritually, it means to apostatize or to stray away from the covenant with God.

▶ "Adultery," the English word, comes from the Latin *ad*, which means "to" and *alter*, which means "other, different" (to make different, to alter).

▶ "Adultery" in Hebrew is the word *naaph*, which is first mentioned in the Bible, the seventh of God's Ten Commandments.[2]

> **"You shall not commit adultery."**
> **(Exodus 20:14)**

Misplaced Attraction

QUESTION: "I find myself attracted to someone other than my wife. What can I do to ensure that I will be faithful?"

ANSWER: At the very moment your emotions start turning from your wife to someone else, redirect your mind and emotions back to your wife. Realize that guardrails on mountain roads serve as constraints that compel us to stay on course and drive safely. They keep us from plunging off the road to destruction below. In the same way, guarding your emotions keeps you from plunging headlong into an adulterous affair.

Pray ...

"Lord, I refuse to let my mind get off course. I choose to guard my mind. I will focus on being faithful to my marriage commitment, my spouse, and my Savior. In Your strength I pray, Amen."

"Let your eyes look straight ahead;
fix your gaze directly before you.
Give careful thought to the paths for your
feet and be steadfast in all your ways. Do
not turn to the right or the left;
keep your foot from evil."
(Proverbs 4:25–27)

Two marriage covenants have now been stained, sullied by a man who should have modeled God's command rather than manipulate the tempting scene to satisfy his lust.

Those who commit adultery will be held accountable according to God's Word, and that extends even to God's anointed David. He will face a lifetime of tragic consequences because he allowed a casual glance across a courtyard to turn into unlawful lust. And not only has David tarnished his own integrity, but he has also cast a dark shadow over God's holy reputation among the nations—for that, too, he will be judged.

All too soon, David will hear a harsh rebuke through the prophet Nathan:

> " ... by doing this you have shown utter contempt for the LORD."
> (2 Samuel 12:14)

▶ **To adulterate** is to corrupt or debase.

▶ **To adulterate** is to make impure or inferior by adding something improper.

▶ **To adulterate** sexually means to be involved in any sexually impure activity.

> "Among you there must not be even a hint of sexual immorality, or of any kind of impurity." (Ephesians 5:3)

Prayer for an Adulterous Husband

QUESTION: "How should I pray for my husband, who has left me and is involved in an adulterous relationship?"

ANSWER: Your husband needs to feel heavy conviction so that he will want to turn from his unfaithful lifestyle. Rather than praying for God to bless him, pray for him to become a faithful husband, a man of integrity who has God's favor.

Pray ...

▶ That your husband can't help but be miserable because of his betrayal

▶ That he would have a heaviness of heart and piercing guilt

▶ That he would be driven out of the arms of this other woman and into the arms of God

▶ That God will use whatever sorrow is necessary to bring him back to his senses

▶ That God will withhold blessings from him until he repents

> **"Repent, then, and turn to God,**
> **so that your sins may be wiped out,**
> **that times of refreshing**
> **may come from the Lord."**
> **(Acts 3:19)**

David's adultery will snowball into a host of other sins, all designed to cover up what is due to come in nine months—*a baby*. Bathsheba returns home following their one-night tryst, and David may have thought he'd "gotten away with it." But a short message—just three words long—forever changes his life: *"I am pregnant"* (2 Samuel 11:5). Now with an illegitimate child surely on the way, David's thoughts turn to one vital person—*the husband of Bathsheba*.

His mind spins; somehow he must bring Uriah home from battle to sleep with her so that the baby will appear to be his. After David sends word to his commander to send Uriah home, David plans to give him perfect marching orders, but the honorable Uriah will not march to David's drum.

Indeed that one night of fornication will result in fearful guilt. One day David will say ...

> **"My guilt has overwhelmed me like a burden too heavy to bear." (Psalm 38:4)**

▶ "Fornication" is generally an umbrella word for any sexual immorality, including adultery and pornographic acts. The Greek word *porneia*, from which we get the English word *pornography*, is often translated "fornication."[3]

13

- ▶ Fornication sometimes refers to sexual intercourse between two unmarried persons.

- ▶ Fornication is used as a spiritual metaphor when referring to mixing worldliness and godliness.

> "Now the body is not for fornication,
> but for the Lord,
> and the Lord for the body."
> (1 Corinthians 6:13 KJV)

Reconciling After Numerous Affairs

QUESTION: "My husband had numerous affairs and now wants to reconcile. Should we get back together?"

ANSWER: Ask yourself this question: What would make me think I can trust him now when I couldn't trust him in the past? The past is the best predictor of the future unless some kind of intervention occurs. Negative patterns rarely change, although the Lord can certainly change anyone who is willing to give Him total control. God is a God of reconciliation, but reconciliation takes two people, not just one.

Until you are thoroughly convinced by both his attitudes and actions that he has indeed changed, do not give open access to your home, your children, your heart, or your bed.

You need substantial reasons to think he is now trustworthy and ready to commit to the marriage.

Ask these key questions to help determine whether or not your husband has indeed changed:

▶ Is he genuinely repentant?

▶ Is he taking personal responsibility for his immoral behavior?

▶ Has he stopped blaming you?

▶ Has he sought counsel to understand his wayward behavior?

▶ Is he willing to be tested for sexually transmitted diseases and disclose the results to you?

▶ Does he have *sacrificial* love for you, not just physical or emotional love?

▶ Is he unquestionably committed to keeping the marriage covenant?

▶ Is he demonstrating respect for you even when you don't agree?

"Husbands ... be considerate
as you live with your wives,
and treat them with respect as the weaker
partner and as heirs with you
of the gracious gift of life."
(1 Peter 3:7)

The seriousness of adultery is seen through God's prohibition in the Ten Commandments, as well as in Jesus' warning, "... *anyone who looks at a woman lustfully has already committed adultery with her in his heart*" (Matthew 5:28).

God designed sexuality to be practiced and enjoyed within the context of marriage—a lifelong commitment between a man and a woman as the embodiment of purity and loyalty.

CHARACTERISTICS OF ONE DRAWN INTO ADULTERY

David hardly seems like the same man that the prophet Samuel anointed with oil and designated as Israel's next king. Years before, the sons of Jesse were paraded before Samuel. Although he was most impressed with the kingly appearance of the eldest son, God's assessment was altogether different. One by one God rejected all seven brothers, prompting Samuel to inquire of the father: *"Are these all the sons you have?" "'There is still the youngest,' Jesse answered. 'He is tending the sheep'"* (1 Samuel 16:11).

Indeed it was the shepherd boy that God chose to sit on the throne of Israel, and He explained to Samuel why: *"The LORD does not look at the things people look at. People look at the outward appearance, but the LORD looks at the heart"* (1 Samuel 16:7).

But the heart once humble before God is now hardened by his own infidelity. Scripture warns about the dangers of a hardened heart:

"Blessed is the one who always trembles before God, but whoever hardens their heart falls into trouble." (Proverbs 28:14)

The outer signs of David's adultery are encapsulated in one word—*cover-up*.

Uriah and David meet, and the king puts his plan into motion with polite conversation. After they chitchat about the challenges of war, David issues a casual directive: *"Go down to your house and wash your feet"* (2 Samuel 11:8).

The king isn't telling Uriah to bathe—he's encouraging him, according to an idiom of the day, to have sex with his wife. David may breathe a sigh of relief as he watches Uriah leave his presence, but the noble warrior never leaves the palace premises. He chooses instead to sleep alongside the king's servants at the entrance to the palace guarding the king, *honoring David*.

The next day David asks Uriah why he didn't go home. Uriah respectfully responds, *"my commander Joab and my lord's men are camped in the open country. How could I go to my house to eat and drink and make love to my wife? As surely as you live, I will not do such a thing!"* (2 Samuel 11:11).

But David, slipping deeper into desperation, will do all he can to make sure Uriah certainly does *"such a thing"*! He gets Uriah drunk, thinking dulled senses will diminish his sense of duty. But the following night, Uriah is found once again sleeping among the king's servants.

And so David spirals even deeper into the depths of sin, making this confession.

> "Troubles without number surround me;
> my sins have overtaken me,
> and I cannot see.
> They are more than the hairs of my head,
> and my heart fails within me."
> (Psalm 40:12)

Possible Outer Signs of Adultery

▶ Change in behavior

▶ Change in mood

▶ Change in spending patterns

▶ Change in schedule

▶ Changes in physical appearance (clothing, jewelry, fragrances)

▶ Less personal conversation

▶ Less vulnerability in sharing

▶ Less discussion of future plans

▶ Less spontaneity

▶ Less sexual intimacy

▶ More out-of-town "business" trips

▶ More unaccounted time away from home

- ▶ More fault-finding

- ▶ More emotional distance

- ▶ More unexpected gifts ("guilt gifts")

- ▶ More anger at being questioned

Justification. Excuses. Rationalization. Those who have illicit affairs are quick to "spin the truth" in order to cover their tracks, yet this biblical proverb presents an eye-opening perspective.

> **"Whoever walks in integrity walks securely, but whoever takes crooked paths will be found out."**
> **(Proverbs 10:9)**

Protection from the Adulterer's Debt

QUESTION: "What can I do about my husband's spending a great deal of money on a girlfriend whom he is living with and incurring large amounts of debt?"

ANSWER: Consult an attorney who specializes in family or consumer law to learn about your legal options within the area where you reside. The laws vary from state-to-state or country-to-country regarding how a spouse can protect financial interests when the other spouse is incurring debts on joint credit cards. In a "common law" state, you may be able to protect yourself from a spouse's debt, but in a "community property" state your assets and debt are normally united.[4]

> **"Plans are established by seeking advice ... obtain guidance."**
> **(Proverbs 20:18)**

WHAT ARE the Characteristics of Adulterous Temptation?

The forbidden fruit—the temptation to taste. Oh, but it's acting on the temptation that sours the sweet fellowship David once had with his Lord.

What has become of the man once after God's own heart, the man who now refuses to heed the dictates of Scripture, who now chooses to pursue temporal pleasures over eternal treasures?

Scripture warns ...

> **"So, if you think you are standing firm,**
> **be careful that you don't fall!**
> **No temptation has overtaken you**
> **except what is common to mankind.**
> **And God is faithful; he will not let you be**
> **tempted beyond what you can bear.**
> **But when you are tempted,**
> **he will also provide a way out**
> **so that you can endure it."**
> **(1 Corinthians 10:12–13)**

David is now "swallowed up" by sin, consumed not with the things of God but with the mechanics of manipulation—how to "solve" his problem once and for all. And so, in coldhearted calculation, David sends Uriah back to the battlefield with note in hand directing Joab to ensure his demise. *"Put Uriah out in front where the fighting is fiercest. Then withdraw from him so he will be struck down and die"* (2 Samuel 11:15). The words penned by the hand of David are inconceivably cruel.

Adultery, deception, manipulation, and now *murder* are among King David's sins, for Uriah does indeed die on the battlefield. But what David has ignored or foolishly forgotten is that ...

**"Nothing in all creation is hidden
from God's sight. Everything is uncovered
and laid bare before the eyes
of him to whom we must give account."
(Hebrews 4:13)**

Typical Adulterous Temptation

The following is an acrostic using the word *TEMPTATION.*

T **ASTING** the forbidden
  LURED by the eyes

E **MOTIONAL** enticements
  FOCUSING on lustful feelings

M **INIMIZES** the marriage
  DEVALUING the marriage commitment

P **HYSICAL** absence
  AVOIDING home and family

T **RADING** priorities
  CHOOSING pleasure over principle

A **NGER** over accountability
  REFUSING to discuss marriage problems

T **WISTING** the truth
  LYING about the affair

I **MAGINING** the impure
  FIXATED on fantasy thinking

O **BSESSED** devotion
  DEFENDING and justifying the "third party"

N **EGLECTING** righteous ways
  HARDENING the heart toward God

"When tempted, no one should say, 'God is tempting me.' For God cannot be tempted by evil, nor does he tempt anyone."
(James 1:13)

QUESTION: "Why does anyone get involved in adultery?"

ANSWER: While there may be a variety of reasons why a person would get involved in adultery, we must acknowledge that the root of the problem begins when the marriage covenant is not honored. When boundaries begin to waver and when compromises are made, anyone can become ensnared by adultery. In Matthew 5:27–28, Jesus Himself makes it clear that adultery begins with the eyes when He says, *"You shall not commit adultery. But I tell you that anyone who looks at a woman lustfully has already committed adultery with her in his heart."*

Scripture also tells us through John that the snare of adultery is not from God when he said, *"For everything in the world — the lust of the flesh, the lust of the eyes, and the pride of life — comes not from the father but from the world"* (1 John 2:16).

**"I will be careful to lead a blameless life ...
I will not look with approval
on anything that is vile."
(Psalm 101:2–3)**

Once again ominous words surround the actions of King David. For a brief period he thinks all the problems are solved. Uriah is dead, and Bathsheba is David's—she becomes his wife and bears him a son. *"But the thing David had done displeased the LORD"* (2 Samuel 11:27).

God's Perspective from Proverbs Chapter 6

▶ **Adulterers** are smooth talkers.

" ... correction and instruction are the way to life, keeping you from your neighbor's wife, from the smooth talk of a wayward woman" (Proverbs 6:23–24).

▶ **Adulterers** play with fire and get burned.

"Can a man scoop fire into his lap without his clothes being burned?" (Proverbs 6:27).

▶ **Adulterers** will be punished.

"So is he who sleeps with another man's wife; no one who touches her will go unpunished" (Proverbs 6:29).

▶ **Adulterers** lack judgment.

"A man who commits adultery has no sense ..." (Proverbs 6:32).

▶ **Adulterers** destroy themselves.

> *"... whoever does so destroys himself"* (Proverbs 6:32).

▶ **Adulterers** will be disgraced.

> *"Blows and disgrace are his lot ..."* (Proverbs 6:33).

▶ **Adulterers** will experience never-ending shame.

> *"... and his shame will never be wiped away"* (Proverbs 6:33).

▶ **Adulterers** evoke anger and jealousy in their spouses.

> *"For jealousy arouses a husband's fury ... "* (Proverbs 6:34).

▶ **Adulterers** often become the object of revenge.

> *"... and he [the husband] will show no mercy when he takes revenge"* (Proverbs 6:34).

For those victimized by adultery, turn to God, seek His guidance, and find hope through a deepened understanding that forgiveness heals wounded hearts and God can restore joy and contentment to your life.

Let this verse be the prayer of your heart:

> "Heal me, LORD, and I will be healed;
> save me and I will be saved,
> for you are the one I praise."
> (Jeremiah 17:14)

CAUSES OF COMMITTING ADULTERY

David, the adulterer, is asked the question directly, *"Why did you despise the word of the LORD by doing what is evil in his eyes?"* (2 Samuel 12:9).

This piercing inquiry is intended to stir the spirit of a man operating in the fullness of the flesh. Not only are David's actions characterized as evil, his disobedience displays disdain for the commandments of Scripture. David is silent as God, through the prophet Nathan, lists reason after reason why there is simply no excuse for his infidelity.

"I anointed you king over Israel,
and I delivered you from the hand of Saul. I
gave your master's house to you,
and your master's wives into your arms.
I gave you all Israel and Judah.
And if all this had been too little,
I would have given you even more."
(2 Samuel 12:7–8)

When confronted by God, David is no doubt filled with self-disdain for his sinful downfall.

Scripture doesn't reveal why King David didn't go to war with his army, as was custom, or why he paced the rooftop of his palace that restless evening. But his actions hint that his flesh may have been inflamed because his spiritual fire was waning. In all likelihood, if David had been conversing with God on that rooftop—immersed in praising and petitioning his Lord—he would not have been deceived and ensnared by adultery.

But on that fateful night, perhaps David believed an adulterous encounter would meet his needs rather than relying on intimate fellowship with God. And now, with Nathan's finger pointing squarely at him, David realizes just how deceived he has been. He experiences firsthand a sobering truth in Scripture:

> " ... you may be sure that your sin
> will find you out."
> (Numbers 32:23)

Adultery is so deceptive because it ...

▶ **Distorts** objectivity

▶ **Gives** an illusion of being loved

▶ **Feels** good physically

▶ **Numbs** emotional pain

▶ **Makes** both parties feel wanted

▶ **Gives** a false sense of significance

▶ **Gives** a false feeling of connecting

▶ **Provides** a temporary sense of security

▶ **Diverts** attention away from family problems

Adultery deceptively promises happiness but leads to bondage. Only truth is liberating.

> "Then you will know the truth,
> and the truth will set you free."
> (John 8:32)

When You're Suspicious

QUESTION: "Is it wrong to try to find out whether or not my spouse is being unfaithful? If it's not wrong, what is the best way to do so?"

ANSWER: It's not wrong to search out and confirm the truth. Truth sets us free to make wise choices regarding the future. When a question of fidelity arises ...

▶ The first approach is to confront your marriage partner with specific concerns.

▶ Afterward, if you are still unsettled in your spirit, pray about approaches that others have used successfully.

▶ Some have spoken with a close friend, a coworker, or a discerning family member of the spouse, specifically asking if they are aware of any romantic involvement outside the marriage.

▶ Still others hire a private investigator.

Before you do anything, pray for God to reveal the truth to you and ask Him to lead you down the path of His choosing.

> **"Whether you turn to the**
> **right or to the left,**
> **your ears will hear a voice behind you,**
> **saying, 'This is the way; walk in it.'"**
> **(Isaiah 30:21)**

WHY ARE People Drawn into Adultery?

Every step David takes toward Bathsheba is a step away from God. By being drawn into adultery, David learns a bitter lesson about meeting his legitimate needs *illegitimately*.

Those few encounters of forbidden passion result in far-reaching consequences, and ultimately David has no control over what happens to his newborn son. Most likely, pregnancy wasn't on David's mind during his throes of passion, nor was the possibility of the death of their firstborn child on his seventh day of life. In truth, God considers David's infidelity an affront against Him personally. He said ...

> " ... you despised me and took the wife of Uriah the Hittite to be your own."
> (2 Samuel 12:10)

When asked "Why were you drawn into adultery?" the response is almost always among these answers:

▶ **"I focused** on what I thought would meet my needs."

▶ **"I blamed** my marriage partner for my problems."

▶ **"I rationalized**: God understands my situation."

▶ **"I failed** to look at the lifelong consequences."

▶ **"I assumed** my mate would never change."

▶ **"I believed** it would make me happy."

▶ **"I opened** the door of compromise."

▶ **"I thought** I wouldn't be caught."

▶ **"I hardened** my heart."

▶ **"I was lured** by lust."

The Bible refers to those whose boundaries have been blurred by unrestrained sensuality:

> "Having lost all sensitivity,
> they have given themselves over to
> sensuality so as to indulge in every kind of
> impurity, and they are full of greed."
> (Ephesians 4:19)

Blame Shifting

QUESTION: "I've been pulled back into an affair with a woman I once dated. We were both promiscuous then, but I hate the deception now. Why would this woman from my past devalue my marriage now?"

ANSWER: Be aware of your wording. The "blame game" is powerfully effective in shifting blame to someone else. In truth, you know right from wrong. The bigger question is:

▶ Why would you walk into a lion's cage with a warning sign that says, "Beware, man-eating lion!"?

▶ You walked back into the relationship, totally ignoring the knowledge you possess and are now being eaten up by your lust.

You are the one who devalued your marriage by choosing to ignore the warning sign, and now you are being mauled! Get out immediately, slam the door, and don't look back. Look at this powerful warning:

> "Don't lust for her beauty.
> Don't let her coy glances seduce you.
> For a prostitute will bring you to poverty,
> but sleeping with another man's wife
> will cost you your life."
> (Proverbs 6:25–26 NLT)

WHAT ARE Reasons to Stop Committing Adultery?

The removal of blessing and the judgment of God are two compellingly powerful reasons to stop committing adultery,

In addition to the death of his newborn son, David's very own household later experiences rape, violence, and murder as a result of his sins. Even one of his sons will seek to dethrone him.

In the end, David's adulterous actions were tied to the Lord's costly consequences.

"You struck down Uriah the Hittite with the sword and took his wife to be your own. ... Now, therefore, the sword will never depart from your house. ... 'Out of your own household I am going to bring calamity on you. Before your very eyes I will take your wives and give them to one who is close to you, and he will sleep with your wives in broad daylight. You did it in secret, but I will do this thing in broad daylight before all Israel'" (2 Samuel 12: 9–12).

No one wants to experience painful repercussions from God. Therefore, anyone who is being unfaithful needs to admit these realities:

▶ "My Bible forbids it."

▶ "My mate is wounded."

▶ "My peace is forfeited."

▶ "My health is jeopardized."

▶ "My future will not be blessed."

▶ "My morality is compromised."

▶ "My children lose their hero."

▶ "My conscience is scarred."

▶ "My integrity is destroyed."

▶ "My God condemns it."

> **"The integrity of the upright guides them, but the unfaithful are destroyed by their duplicity." (Proverbs 11:3)**

Disrespectful Treatment

QUESTION: "I caught my husband cheating on me. He often treated me disrespectfully before we were married. Why would he do this to me?"

ANSWER: Realize that a disrespectful date will be a disrespectful mate. It is as though you saw a warning sign reading, "Quicksand," yet you kept walking straight ahead and now you are shocked that you are sinking. So what do you do now? Rather than asking why he is disrespectful toward you, ask yourself why you tolerated any disrespect from him in the first place.

▶ Rather than being shocked at your husband's behavior, consider why you were attracted to and then married someone who treated you disrespectfully.

▶ Rather than trying to understand the motivation behind his actions, seek to understand the motivation behind your own actions.

▶ Rather than trying to change him, change yourself.

Remember, if you want to be respected, don't tolerate being disrespected. And regardless of the reason for his decision to cheat, you have a decision to make regarding his choice. If you want him to respect you, then you need to decide to respect yourself enough to set firm boundaries on what you will not tolerate. Then get an accountability partner who will help you maintain those boundaries.

> **"Above all else, guard your heart,**
> **for everything you do flows from it."**
> **(Proverbs 4:23)**

David's restlessness should have led him before the throne of God rather than into the bed of another man's wife. The peace he lacked and the joy he sought would have been given to him by the Lord, but David chose a counterfeit path—a path that promised pleasure but in the end produced pain.

David should have recalled the words he himself wrote when he lived dependently on the Lord.

"The LORD is my shepherd; I shall not want." (Psalm 23:1 NKJV)

Three God-Given Inner Needs

In reality, we have all been created with three God-given inner needs: the needs for love, significance, and security.[5]

▶ **Love**—to know that someone is unconditionally committed to our best interest

"My command is this: Love each other as I have loved you" (John 15:12).

▶ **Significance**—to know that our lives have meaning and purpose

"I cry out to God Most High, to God who fulfills his purpose for me" (Psalm 57:2 ESV).

▶**Security**—to feel accepted and a sense of belonging

"Whoever fears the Lord has a secure fortress, and for their children it will be a refuge" (Proverbs 14:26).

The Ultimate Need-Meeter

Why did God give us these deep inner needs, knowing that people fail people and self-effort fails us as well?

God gave us these inner needs so that we would come to know Him as our Need-Meeter. Our needs are designed by God to draw us into a deeper dependence on Christ. God did not create any person or position, or any amount of power or possessions to meet the deepest needs in our lives. If a person or thing could meet all our needs, we wouldn't need God! The Lord will use circumstances and bring positive people into our lives as an extension of His care and compassion, but ultimately only God can satisfy all the needs of our hearts.

The Bible says ...

"The LORD will guide you always;
he will satisfy your needs in a sun-scorched
land and will strengthen your frame.
You will be like a well-watered garden,
like a spring whose waters never fail."
(Isaiah 58:11)

The apostle Paul revealed this truth by first asking, *"What a wretched man I am. Who will rescue me from this body that is subject to death?"* and then by answering his own question in saying it is *"Jesus Christ our Lord!"* (Romans 7:24–25).

All along, the Lord planned to meet our deepest needs for ...

▶ **Love**—*"I [the Lord] have loved you with an everlasting love; I have drawn you with unfailing kindness"* (Jeremiah 31:3).

▶ **Significance**—*"'For I know the plans I have for you,' declares the LORD, 'plans to prosper you and not to harm you, plans to give you hope and a future'"* (Jeremiah 29:11).

▶ **Security**—*"The LORD himself goes before you and will be with you; he will never leave you nor forsake you. Do not be afraid; do not be discouraged"* (Deuteronomy 31:8).

The truth is that our God-given needs for love, significance, and security can be legitimately met in Christ Jesus! Philippians 4:19 makes it plain: *"My God will meet all your needs according to the riches of his glory in Christ Jesus."*

Ultimately, the root cause of adultery is the spiritual and emotional immaturity of one or both marriage partners who become unwilling to keep their personal commitment to their marriage.

► **WRONG BELIEF:** "I have a right to get my basic needs for love, significance, and security met. I don't feel that my previous commitments are binding because my mate isn't meeting all my needs."

"Marriage should be honored by all, and the marriage bed kept pure, for God will judge the adulterer and all the sexually immoral" (Hebrews 13:4).

► **RIGHT BELIEF:** "My deepest inner needs will be completely met in a genuine relationship with Jesus, who will be faithful to fulfill me. As I give myself to Christ and obey His commands, He will give me the right desires and the ability to remain faithful to my commitment to my mate."

"Take delight in the LORD, and he will give you the desires of your heart. Commit your way to the Lord; trust in him and he will do this" (Psalm 37:4–5).

Unmet Emotional Needs

QUESTION: "My mate has abandoned me. What am I to do about getting my emotional needs met?"

ANSWER: Your emotional needs are God-given and legitimate. And God will prove Himself faithful to you by meeting those needs if you will seek His provision. Trust Him to meet your emotional needs in His time and in His way.

"The righteous cry out, and the LORD hears them; he delivers them from all their troubles. The LORD is close to the brokenhearted and saves those who are crushed in spirit."
(Psalm 34:17–18)

How Can I Have a Genuine Relationship with Christ?

There are four spiritual truths you need to know.

Four Points of God's Plan:

#1 God's Purpose for You is *Salvation*.

What was God's motivation in sending Jesus Christ to earth?

To express His love for you by saving you!

The Bible says ...

"God so loved the world that he gave his one and only Son, that whoever believes in him shall not perish but have eternal life. For God did not send his Son into the world to condemn the world, but to save the world through him" (John 3:16–17).

What was Jesus' purpose in coming to earth?

To forgive your sins, to empower you to have victory over sin, and to enable you to live a fulfilled life!

Jesus said ...

"I have come that they may have life, and that they may have it more abundantly." (John 10:10 NKJV)

#2 Your Problem is *Sin.*

What exactly is sin?

Sin is living independently of God's standard—knowing what is right, but choosing what is wrong.

The Bible says ...

"If anyone, then, knows the good they ought to do and doesn't do it, it is sin for them" (James 4:17).

What is the major consequence of sin?

Spiritual death, eternal separation from God. Scripture states …

"Your iniquities [sins] have separated you from your God" (Isaiah 59:2).

"The wages of sin is death, but the gift of God is eternal life in Christ Jesus our Lord" (Romans 6:23).

#3 God's Provision for You is the *Savior.*

Can anything remove the penalty for sin?

Yes! Jesus died on the cross to personally pay the penalty for your sins.

The Bible says …

"God demonstrates his own love for us in this: While we were still sinners, Christ died for us" (Romans 5:8).

What is the solution to being separated from God?

Belief in (entrusting your life to) Jesus Christ as the only way to God the Father.

Jesus says …

"I am the way and the truth and the life. No one comes to the Father except through me" (John 14:6).

Believe in the Lord Jesus, and you will be saved ..." (Acts 16:31).

#4 Your Part is *Surrender.*

Give Christ control of your life, entrusting yourself to Him.

"Jesus said to his disciples, 'Whoever wants to be my disciple must deny themselves and take up their cross [die to your own self-rule] and follow me. For whoever wants to save their life will lose it, but whoever loses their life for me will find it. What good will it be for someone to gain the whole world, yet forfeit their soul?'" (Matthew 16:24–26).

Place your faith in (rely on) Jesus Christ as your personal Lord and Savior and reject your "good works" as a means of earning God's approval.

"It is by grace you have been saved, through faith—and this is not from yourselves, it is the gift of God—not by works, so that no one can boast" (Ephesians 2:8–9).

The moment you choose to receive Jesus as your Lord and Savior—entrusting your life to Him—He comes to live inside you. Then He gives you His power to live the fulfilled life God has planned for you. If you want to be fully forgiven by God and become the person God created you to be, you can tell Him in a simple, heartfelt prayer like this:

PRAYER OF SALVATION

"God, I want a real relationship with You. I admit that many times I've chosen to go my own way instead of Your way. Please forgive me for my sins. Jesus, thank You for dying on the cross to pay the penalty for my sins. Come into my life to be my Lord and my Savior. Help me to depend on You alone to meet my needs. Through Your power, make me the person You created me to be. In Your holy name I pray. Amen."

What Can You Expect Now?

If you sincerely prayed this prayer, look at what God says!

"His divine power has given us everything we need for a godly life through our knowledge of him who called us by his own glory and goodness. Through these he has given us his very great and precious promises, so that through them you may participate in the divine nature, having escaped the corruption in the world caused by evil desires."
(2 Peter 1:3–4)

Reconnection with God

QUESTION: "My husband is my life, yet he is involved in an adulterous relationship. I am consumed with pain and unable to read the Bible or pray. How can I connect with God mentally and emotionally? I need Him desperately."

ANSWER: No human being is ever to be our "life." God wants you to yield your will to His will and allow Jesus to take control of your life. As a Christian, Jesus Christ is your life. Make Him the foundation of your life, and He will provide you with emotional and mental stability.

"He will be the sure foundation for your times, a rich store of salvation and wisdom and knowledge; the fear of the LORD is the key to this treasure."
(Isaiah 33:6)

STEPS TO SOLUTION

Just before the prophet Nathan confronts David about his adultery, he primes David's heart with a parable so that he will feel the full weight of his sin. Nathan describes two men to David, one who is rich with a large number of sheep and cattle, and the other a poor man with nothing of value except a little ewe he nurtures like a daughter.

A traveler requests a meal from the rich man, and rather than slaughter a sheep or cow from his giant herds, he kills the poor man's pet sheep. David's anger flares and he vows: *"As surely as the LORD lives, the man who did this must die! He must pay for that lamb four times over, because he did such a thing and had no pity"* (2 Samuel 12:5–6).

Then Nathan raises his finger toward David: *"You are the man!"* (2 Samuel 12:7).

Key Verses to Memorize

When it comes to adultery or any form of sexual immorality, the Bible has a very clear command: *flee*.

▶ **For the unfaithful partner:** *"Flee from sexual immorality. All other sins a person commits are outside the body, but whoever*

sins sexually, sins against their own body"
(1 Corinthians 6:18).

If there is even a hint or an inkling that adultery may be creeping into our lives, Scripture tells us to run in the opposite direction. Sexual sins are uniquely devastating because the immoral sin is against their own bodies, while all other sins are committed outside the body.

▶ **For the faithful partner**: *"For your Maker is your husband—the LORD Almighty is his name—the Holy One of Israel is your Redeemer; he is called the God of all the earth"* (Isaiah 54:5).

For the spouse who has been wounded by unfaithfulness, always remember there is Someone who stands by your side faithful and true. He will never reject you. He will never leave you.

God is mighty, fully able to meet your needs and to bring about healing and reconciliation even in the darkest, most desperate situations.

Key Passage to Read

The Bible prescribes an even more forceful command concerning the drive or desire to be sexually immoral—*kill it.*

Sexual sins, like many other sins, can become all-consuming, preoccupying our thoughts and time until our behavior is nothing short of idolatrous. And idolatry, according to Scripture, prompts a serious and sobering response from God—divine punishment.

▶ **For the unfaithful partner**,
read Colossians 3:1–15.

> **"Put to death, therefore,**
> **whatever belongs to your earthly nature:**
> **sexual immorality, impurity, lust,**
> **evil desires and greed, which is idolatry.**
> **Because of these,**
> **the wrath of God is coming."**
> **(Colossians 3:5–6)**

A natural response from those deeply wounded by an adulterous spouse is to seek revenge for all the pain that now characterizes the fractured relationship.

But God calls the faithful partner to respond supernaturally, to forgive and allow God to administer justice. It's important to remember that forgiveness doesn't always include reconciliation. Pray and follow God's leading as to whether the marriage should continue.

▶ **For the faithful partner**,
read Romans 12:9–21.

> **"Do not take revenge, my dear friends,**
> **but leave room for God's wrath,**
> **for it is written: 'It is mine to avenge;**
> **I will repay,' says the Lord."**
> **(Romans 12:19)**

The parable—along with a divine proclamation of a painful slew of judgments—grip David's spirit and lead to a grievous confession: *"I have sinned against the LORD"* (2 Samuel 12:13).

Psalm 51 records the outpouring of David's heart as he fully acknowledges his sins before God—recognizing that ultimately they are committed against Him. He pleads for mercy, forgiveness, purity of heart, and steadfastness of spirit. *Crushing* is how David describes the weightiness of his conviction, and he longs for the burden to be lifted. He longs to be changed—for good.

David's heart cry is ...

> **"Create in me a pure heart, O God,
> and renew a steadfast spirit within me. ...
> Restore to me the joy of your salvation
> and grant me a willing spirit, to sustain me."
> (Psalm 51:10, 12)**

1 **Confess** the adultery.

▶ **Don't think,** "I'll put the affair behind me. No one needs to know."

▶ **Decide now** that the truth must come out in order for God to bring healing.

"Confess your sins to each other and pray for each other so that you may be healed" (James 5:16).

2 Commit yourself to your covenant partner completely.

▶ **Don't think,** "Children are the glue in marriage."

▶ **Decide now** that commitment is the glue that holds a marriage together.

" ... the LORD is the witness between you and the wife of your youth. You have been unfaithful to her, though she is your partner, the wife of your marriage covenant. Has not the one God made you? You belong to him in body and spirit. And what does the one God seek? Godly offspring. So be on your guard, and do not be unfaithful to the wife of your youth" (Malachi 2:14–15).

3 Cut all ties with the third party.

▶ **Don't think,** "Affairs are okay as long as no one knows."

▶ **Decide now** that adultery cannot be hidden. God knows, the illicit partner knows, and in time, others know. Ultimately, the affair will burn you.

"Can a man walk on hot coals without his feet being scorched?" (Proverbs 6:28).

4 Choose where to place your thoughts when tempted.

▶ **Don't think,** "All I am doing is admiring the beauty of God's creation! What's wrong with that?"

▶ **Decide now** that I cannot fool God. I will honor and protect my marriage covenant by my thoughts and actions, and His peace will be with me.

"Finally, brothers and sisters, whatever is true, whatever is noble, whatever is right, whatever is pure, whatever is lovely, whatever is admirable—if anything is excellent or praiseworthy—think about such things. Whatever you have learned or received or heard from me, or seen in me— put it into practice. And the God of peace will be with you" (Philippians 4:8-9).

5 Consider the difference between love and lust.

▶ **Don't think,** "How can it be so wrong if it feels so right?"

▶ **Decide now** that love is not a feeling. The supreme test to determine if something is right is not how it feels, but what God says about it. If sin never felt good, no one would ever be tempted to sin. Love is a choice to make a personal sacrifice.

"Husbands, love your wives, just as Christ loved the church and gave himself up for her" (Ephesians 5:25).

6 Count the cost.

▶ **Don't think,** "As long as no one knows, no one is hurt."

▶ **Decide now** that adultery hurts everyone involved. You've brought guilt and God's judgment not only on yourself, but also on the other person.

"The trouble they cause recoils on them ... " (Psalm 7:16).

7 Communicate godly sorrow.

▶ **Don't think,** "If I admit I'm sorry about the affair, everything will be okay."

▶ **Decide now** that there is a vast difference between "worldly sorrow" and "godly sorrow." Worldly sorrow is being sorry for getting caught. Godly sorrow is a change of mind with a change of direction, resulting in a change of behavior. You hate your sin so much that you turn from it and never turn back to it again.

"Godly sorrow brings repentance that leads to salvation and leaves no regret, but worldly sorrow brings death" (2 Corinthians 7:10).

Rebuilding Trust

QUESTION: "My husband, who sexually betrayed me, blames me for not trusting him. What should I do?"

ANSWER: Trust cannot be demanded—it must be earned. He must prove himself *over time* to be trustworthy. Even Jesus would not trust certain people because He knew what was in their hearts. *"Jesus would not entrust himself to them, for he knew all people"* (John 2:24).

Just like Jesus, you need to be wise and discerning. When trust has been broken, only repentance, faithfulness, and time can fully rebuild trust.

> "It is required that those who have been given a trust must prove faithful."
> (1 Corinthians 4:2)

Painful feelings, wounded hearts, and bruised egos can lead to faithful mates making common mistakes that ignite an emotional tinderbox.

Faithful mates struggling with unfaithfulness in their lives can avoid pitfalls so that peace, healing, and reconciliation occur far more quickly. Lean on the Lord—who will *never* be unfaithful—for wisdom and strength in restoring your relationship. And cling to God's promises in Scripture.

"For the word of the LORD is right and true; he is faithful in all he does."
(Psalm 33:4)

▶ **Don't keep** trying to change your mate.

- You are not responsible for changing your mate. In fact, you *can't* change your mate—you don't have that power.

  "The LORD will fight for you; you need only to be still" (Exodus 14:14).

▶ **Don't repeatedly** bring up the past in order to convict your mate.

- The Holy Spirit is the One who convicts.

  "When he comes, he will prove the world to be in the wrong about sin and righteousness and judgment" (John 16:8).

▶ **Don't blame** yourself for the adultery.[8]

- Almost all wounded mates struggle with false guilt, feeling responsible for the mate's affair. However, whatever you did or didn't do did not cause your spouse to sin against you. You can't make another person sin. Our actions are based on our own individual choices.

  "Each of us will give an account of ourselves to God" (Romans 14:12).

▶ **Don't minimize** or deny the seriousness of the situation.

- Minimizing or denying the seriousness of the situation does not change the fact that it is wrong. Be willing to see sin for what it is.

  "Do not offer any part of yourself to sin as an instrument of wickedness, but rather offer yourselves to God as those who have been brought from death to life; and offer every part of yourself to him as an instrument of righteousness" (Romans 6:13).

▶ **Don't seek** to meet all your mate's needs.

- You can never meet all your mate's needs. If you could meet all those needs, your mate would never need God. He did not create anyone to meet all the needs of another person. Especially beware of becoming another person's god—taking the place that God alone should have. God promises to meet all our needs.

"My God will meet all your needs according to the riches of his glory in Christ Jesus" (Philippians 4:19).

▶ **Don't communicate** that you can't make it alone and that you are completely dependent on your partner.

- Your hope is to be in the Lord alone, not in another person.

"Yes, my soul, find rest in God; my hope comes from him. Truly he is my rock and my salvation; he is my fortress, I will not be shaken. My salvation and my honor depend on God; he is my mighty rock, my refuge" (Psalm 62:5–7).

Feeling Helpless and Hopeless

QUESTION: "My husband is having an affair and refuses to talk about it. He just goes on living as though nothing is happening. I don't feel I have any value. I cry a lot and feel my world is gone. What can I do about feeling helpless and hopeless?"

ANSWER: Your world is not gone. Although you are powerless to change your husband, you are not powerless to change the way you respond. Whether your husband talks about the affair or not, you decide your course of action and tell him what it is. Don't continue playing the part of the victim.

You have the choice to find your significance and security in the Lord. Even though your husband has abdicated his role as husband through infidelity, the *Lord* promises to be *faithful* to you and to His Word. The Lord knows how to meet your need for love. He promises to be your Provider. The deeper your relationship with Him the more stability you will feel in your heart, and you will find your value in Him.

> "Let us hold unswervingly
> to the hope we profess,
> for he who promised is faithful."
> (Hebrews 10:23)

SIX STEPS for the Faithful Mate

Your spouse has been unfaithful. How does God want you to respond?

You may want to lash out in destructive anger. You may vow you'll never forgive. But *natural* responses will never bring about the benefits of *supernatural* responses rooted in the strength, grace, and wisdom of God.

Follow these steps for the faithful spouse, which give sure and steady direction for the trying days ahead.[9]

The psalmist reminds us ...

"See if there is any offensive way in me,
and lead me in the way everlasting."
(Psalm 139:24)

1 **Confront** your mate if you are suspicious.

- **Many wounded mates wonder**, "Do I say something if I have suspicions?" They assume, "Isn't bringing up the subject putting the thought in my mate's mind?"

- **But the truth is** that bringing up the subject might relieve your thoughts if you learn that your suspicions are unwarranted, or might be a deterrent for your spouse in the future, or might be used by the Holy Spirit to convict your partner. Don't attack. Don't blame.

Ask ...

▶ "Are you romantically involved or even romantically interested in someone else?"

▶ "I feel that you are keeping something from me."

▶ "I feel hurt that your affection has turned from me."

▶ "I need you to be totally honest with me."

The Bible says, *"The righteousness of the blameless makes their paths straight, but the wicked are brought down by their own* wickedness. *The righteousness of the upright delivers them, but the unfaithful are trapped by evil desires"* (Proverbs 11:5-6).

2 Refuse to blame yourself for your partner's adulterous behavior.

- **Many wounded mates wonder,** "Where did I go wrong?" They assume that they have failed their mates. This is a very common belief about infidelity.

- **But the truth is** that a spouse is not responsible for the mate's irresponsible behavior. No one can make another person sin.

  The Lord says, *"I will judge each of you according to your own ways. ... Rid yourselves of all the offenses you have committed, and get a new heart and a new spirit"* (Ezekiel 18:30–32).

3 Express your anger in a nondestructive way.

- **Many wounded mates wonder,** "How can I handle my anger?" They assume, "Anger is always wrong."

- **But the truth is** that anger is a natural response to hurt, injustice, fear, and/or frustration.

  The Bible says, *"Be angry, and do not sin"* (Psalm 4:4 NKJV).

4 Pray that you will be guided by the Spirit of God as to whether you should leave an adulterous marriage.

- **Many wounded mates wonder,** "Must I remain in a marriage with an adulterous mate?" They assume, "I must stay married even if my mate continues to commit adultery."

- **But the truth is** that there are biblical grounds for divorce: marital unfaithfulness (adultery). Jesus does not *demand* divorce in such a case, but rather *permits* it. The following conversation took place with the Jewish leaders:

  "Jesus replied. ... 'I tell you that anyone who divorces his wife, except for sexual immorality, and marries another woman commits adultery'" (Matthew 19:8–9).

5 Lean on the Lord to be your Savior, your Completer, your Healer.

- **Many wounded mates wonder,** "What if my mate never returns to me?" They assume, "In order to be whole, I must have a mate."

- **But the truth is** that one is a *whole* number—not a half, not a fraction. You can be complete in Christ.

The **Bible says,** *"You are complete in Him [Christ]"* (Colossians 2:10 NKJV).

6 Choose, as an act of your will, to forgive.

- **Many wounded mates wonder,** "How can I forgive and forget?" They assume, "You must *forget* in order to forgive."

- **But the truth is** that forgiving is not forgetting. The key is *how* it is remembered. Forgiving is remembering without bitterness, hatred, or resentment.

The **Bible says,** *"Bear with each other and forgive one another if any of you has a grievance against someone. Forgive as the Lord forgave you"* (Colossians 3:13).

Continued Anger after Change

QUESTION: "My wife committed adultery years ago. Although she has truly changed, I continue to have trouble forgiving her for the hurt she caused me. How can I overcome the anger I still feel?"

ANSWER: Don't be dismayed over your anger. The four roots of anger are hurt, injustice, fear, and frustration. Your response is normal because the Bible says ...

"'In your anger do not sin': Do not let the sun go down while you are still angry."
(Ephesians 4:26)

Therefore, you can feel legitimate anger over her betrayal. Every time you feel anger, admit it and then release it; release it as a sacrifice to the Lord.

Pray ...

"Lord, right now I release to You all the anger I feel. I choose to guard my mind from thoughts of past events that You have dealt with and that I have forgiven. Thank You for the changes You have brought about in my wife. Thank You that she is a trustworthy woman, and I choose right now to trust You to continue to work in her life. In the name of Your wonderful Son and my Savior I pray. Amen."

Don't allow your enemy to accuse you of unforgiveness just because of how you may feel. Forgiveness is the ongoing process of forgiving each time the pain comes to mind or each time you think about the one who has hurt you. Forgiveness is a choice you have made, and you must learn to place fact over feelings. Satan, your adversary, has already been defeated.

"The accuser of our brothers and sisters, who accuses them before our God day and night, has been hurled down."
(Revelation 12:10)

David comes back to God and finds that compassion and forgiveness await him.

Despite severe consequences for his sins, there are yet blessings for the contrite king. David and Bathsheba conceive a second son, whom they name Solomon, and *"the LORD loved him"* (2 Samuel 12:24). Solomon one day would be known as being *"greater in riches and wisdom than all the other kings of the earth"* (1 Kings 10:23).

And the heart of David—beset with sin for a season—is repeatedly used by God as a spiritual barometer in measuring the commitment of future kings in Judah and Israel. Following his true repentance, David led an honorable life, one primarily characterized by obedience to God.

To Jeroboam, a later king of Israel, God declares, *"you have not been like my servant David, who kept my commands and followed me with all his heart"* (1 Kings 14:8).

#1 Preparing for the Intervention[10]

"Have nothing to do with the fruitless
deeds of darkness, but rather expose them.
It is shameful even to mention what the
disobedient do in secret.
But everything exposed by the light
becomes visible – and everything that is
illuminated becomes a light. ...
Be very careful, then, how you live—
not as unwise but as wise, making the most
of every opportunity, because the days are
evil." (Ephesians 5: 11–13, 15)

▶ **Give** up all expectations of your spouse,
who may or may not change, and place your
confidence in God.

*"It is better to trust in the Lord than to put
confidence in man"* (Psalm 118:8 NKJV).

▶ **Allow** yourself time to grieve the reality of
your situation.

*"My soul is weary with sorrow; strengthen me
according to your word"* (Psalm 119:28).

▶ **Decide** to detach emotionally from your
spouse's infidelity and respond with patience
and gentleness.

*"Through patience a ruler can be persuaded,
and a gentle tongue can break a bone"*
(Proverbs 25:15).

▶ **Shift** your focus from your spouse's hurtful
behavior to your loving responses.

"The soothing tongue is a tree of life, but a perverse tongue crushes the spirit" (Proverbs 15:4).

▶ **Learn** all you can about the deceptive lures of adultery.

"How much better to get wisdom than gold, to get insight rather than silver!" (Proverbs 16:16).

▶ **Share** with your spouse the effect the infidelity has had on you and on others.

"For there is nothing hidden that will not be disclosed, and nothing concealed that will not be known or brought out into the open" (Luke 8:17).

▶ **Stop** enabling adulterous behavior by ignoring telltale signs or accepting lame excuses.

"Have nothing to do with the fruitless deeds of darkness, but rather expose them" (Ephesians 5:11).

▶ **Express** your feelings with your spouse without accusing and condemning.

"A gentle answer turns away wrath, but a harsh word stirs up anger" (Proverbs 15:1)

"The tongue has the power of life and death" (Proverbs 18:21).

▶ **Pray** with the knowledge that God will work in the life of your spouse and will guard your heart.

"Do not be anxious about anything, but in every situation, by prayer and petition, with thanksgiving, present your requests to God. And the peace of God, which transcends all understanding, will guard your hearts and your minds in Christ Jesus" (Philippians 4:6–7).

#2 Planning the Intervention

The most powerful aspect of a crisis intervention is the group dynamic—*there is power in numbers.* Usually by the time an intervention is arranged, the injured spouse has personally pleaded with the offending spouse to stop the adulterous behavior, but sadly the appeal has fallen on deaf ears. In privacy, others may state their concern, but one by one each plea is dismissed. As individuals they are powerless—as a group they are dynamite. In fact, a group can be empowered by God to move the immovable.

"If your brother or sister sins, go and point out their fault, just between the two of you. If they listen to you, you have won them over. But if they will not listen, take one or two others along, so that 'every matter may be established by the testimony of two or three witnesses.'"
(Matthew 18:15–16)
(Read also Ezekiel 3:18–19.)

▶**Pray** for wisdom and understanding from the Lord.

"The LORD gives wisdom; from his mouth come knowledge and understanding" (Proverbs 2:6).

▶**Educate** yourself regarding various crisis intervention programs and attend meetings on surviving adultery, and marriage enrichment. Read materials on intervention and visit counseling centers.

"The heart of the discerning acquires knowledge, for the ears of the wise seek it out" (Proverbs 18:15).

▶**Call** a counseling office and ask for a referral to a Christian leader trained in marital crisis intervention procedures.

"Plans fail for lack of counsel, but with many advisers they succeed" (Proverbs 15:22).

▶**Meet** with an intervention specialist to plan the approach. Discussion needs to include counseling options, insurance coverage, and the impact of counseling on the entire family.

"Listen to advice and accept discipline, and at the end you will be counted among the wise" (Proverbs 19:20).

▶**Enlist** the aid of key people who have been directly affected by the adultery, those who can attest to its harmful effects on others and are willing to confront. (Consider caring family members, friends, a doctor, an employer, a coworker, or a spiritual leader.)

"A truthful witness saves lives ..."
(Proverbs 14:25).

▶ **Hold** an initial meeting with these key people and a trained leader (in absolute confidentiality and without the person present). Each key person will rehearse with the trained leader what each will say regarding the negative impact of the person's adultery, how it will be said, and in which order each will speak during the confrontation.

"Better is open rebuke than hidden love. Wounds from a friend can be trusted, but an enemy multiplies kisses" (Proverbs 27:5–6).

▶ **Hold** a second meeting, this time with the person present. One at a time, each key confronter should first express genuine love and concern for the person, followed by the rehearsed individualized confrontation.

"The words of the reckless pierce like swords, but the tongue of the wise brings healing" (Proverbs 12:18).

#3 Making the Appeal[11]

▶ **The Personal**

Affirm rather than attack: "I want you to know how much I care about you [or love you] and how terribly concerned I am about you."

"Do not let any unwholesome talk come out of your mouths, but only what is helpful for building others up according to their needs, that it may benefit those who listen" (Ephesians 4:29).

▶ **The Past**

Give recent examples describing specific negative behavior and the hurt it caused you: "Last night when you failed to come home and spend time with me as you used to do, I felt so unimportant to you."

"An honest witness tells the truth ... " (Proverbs 12:17).

Be brief, keeping examples to three or four sentences.

"The one who has knowledge uses words with restraint, and whoever has understanding is even-tempered" (Proverbs 17:27).

▶The Pain

Emphasize the painful impact by using "I" statements: "I was devastated that you failed to make me and your commitment to me a priority."

"The hearts of the wise make their mouths prudent, and their lips promote instruction" (Proverbs 16:23).

▶The Plea

Make a personal plea for your loved one to receive counseling: "I plead with you to get the help you need to break away from this sinful and adulterous relationship. If you are willing, you will gain back my deepest respect."

"Hear now my argument; listen to the pleas of my lips" (Job 13:6).

▶The Plan

Be prepared to implement an immediate plan if counseling is accepted: "You have been accepted into the counseling program at _____

_____,

and _____

have agreed to be your accountability partners."

"In their hearts humans plan their course, but the LORD establishes their steps" (Proverbs 16:9).

▶The Price

Outline specific consequences if counseling is refused: "We cannot allow you to come home or be with our family until you have completely walked away from this adulterous relationship and stopped all contact with the other person."

"Stern discipline awaits anyone who leaves the path; the one who hates correction will die" (Proverbs 15:10).

#4 Knowing the Don'ts of Dialogue

▶**Don't call names**, preach, or be judgmental.

"Whoever derides their neighbor has no sense, but the one who has understanding holds their tongue" (Proverbs 11:12).

▶**Don't argue** if your facts are disputed, and don't come to the defense of your spouse when others are confronting. "I'm sorry if you disagree with me, but my facts have been confirmed." "I'm sure there will be changes in our marriage now that the truth is out in the open."

"The Lord's servant must not be quarrelsome but must be kind to everyone, able to teach, not resentful. Opponents must be gently instructed, in the hope that God will grant

them repentance leading them to a knowledge of the truth, and that they will come to their senses and escape from the trap of the devil, who has taken them captive to do his will" (2 Timothy 2:24–26).

▶ **Don't accept promises** without commitment for immediate action.

"I am really thankful that you understand how I feel, but I need to see some proof that you seriously want to change."

"The simple believe anything, but the prudent give thought to their steps" (Proverbs 14:15).

▶ **Don't give ultimatums** unless you are prepared to follow through on them. Suppose your mate chooses to continue the adulterous relationship and leaves home. However, after being away for only a short time, your spouse says, "I promise to not be unfaithful again. Just let me come back this one time." You would be wise to say, "No, not until you have had individual counseling and we both have been in marriage counseling long enough for the therapist and me to be convinced that both you and I are ready for you to return."

"Let your 'Yes' be 'Yes,' and your 'No,' 'No' ..." (James 5:12 NKJV).

▶ **Don't overreact**—keep your emotions under control.

"Everyone should be quick to listen, slow to speak and slow to become angry, because human anger does not produce the righteousness that God desires" (James 1:19–20).

▶ **Don't shield** your loved one from facing the consequences of marital infidelity.

"No discipline seems pleasant at the time, but painful. Later on, however, it produces a harvest of righteousness and peace for those who have been trained by it" (Hebrews 12:11).

The second meeting concludes with the spouse either immediately terminating the adulterous relationship and entering a counseling and accountability program or experiencing the consequences for refusing treatment.

"Whoever rebukes a person will in the end gain favor rather than one who has a flattering tongue." (Proverbs 28:23)

Natural Consequences

QUESTION: "My husband walked away from our family and has been unfaithful. Now he wants to come back. But when I asked him to be tested for sexually transmitted diseases, he accused me of not being a forgiving and compassionate Christian. He says I'm being punitive—I think I'm being practical. Who is right?"

ANSWER: Your husband is simply using the "blame game" to avoid his responsibility to be tested. He is blaming you instead of blaming himself for putting you in this precarious position.

Insist on his need to accept the proper consequences of his promiscuity: mandatory testing for sexually transmitted diseases. This is necessary for your protection, not to humiliate your spouse.

Consult your doctor before resuming sexual activity, and be certain that you are no longer at risk for contracting a sexually transmitted disease.

Keep your boundaries around sexual intimacy in place. Refuse to be manipulated.

The Bible says ...

> "There is a time for everything,
> and a season for every activity
> under the heavens ... a time to embrace
> and a time to refrain."
> (Ecclesiastes 3:1, 5)

David, the military man and conquering king, was also known for his sensitive side. This melancholy musician wrote poignant psalms with questions that plunge to the depths of the soul.

One of his contemplative psalms conveys this lament: *"My soul is in deep anguish. How long, LORD, how long? Turn, LORD, and deliver me ... "* (Psalm 6:3–4).

Many people struggle with difficult questions after experiencing the pain of adultery. Whether the wandering mate who strayed or the wounded one who stayed, God's Word provides the answers.

"Answer me when I call to you, my righteous God. Give me relief from my distress; have mercy on me and hear my prayer."
(Psalm 4:1)

#1 Staying with an Unfaithful Spouse

QUESTION: "Should I stay with my spouse, who has been unfaithful to me but promises it won't happen again?"

ANSWER: Before you make this decision, ask yourself these questions:

▶ Is this a onetime lack of judgment or a repeated lifestyle?

- If it is a lifestyle, then it is an issue of character.

- If it was a onetime act, then it is a single act of sin.

▶ Did your spouse take responsibility, or blame you or someone else?

▶ Is there true repentance—a godly sorrow—or is there simply sorrow only at being caught?

▶ Has all contact with the adulterous partner been severed?

▶ What has been done to make restitution?

▶ What is your mate doing to avoid straying again?

If recent attitudes and actions are positive, you have the potential for genuine reconciliation and a healthy, productive marriage.

> **"If we confess our sins, he is faithful and just and will forgive us our sins and purify us from all unrighteousness." (1 John 1:9)**

#2 Setting Boundaries

QUESTION: "How do I draw a boundary when my husband is sexually involved with another woman? I want our marriage to work."

ANSWER: Be specific about the boundary—he has certainly crossed the line. You could say:

▶ "I love you, and I have been committed to you. But now it's time for you to make a decision:

- "All boundaries have repercussions and rewards. In the game of football, if you stay within the boundary lines, you get to keep playing."

- "If you step outside the boundary, the penalty is no participation."

- "Because of your sexual involvement with this other woman, you've crossed the boundary."

- "So now, it's your decision: Do you want to discontinue your participation in our family life or not? If you choose our family, you must totally leave her. If you choose her over our family, you must leave our home."

Explain that you are not "kicking him out of the house," but that the decision for leaving is completely his choice. You could say, "For you to be emotionally or sexually involved with another woman says that you are not committed to our marriage."

This marriage boundary gives him the choice as to whether he reaps the repercussion or the reward.

For him to continue in the affair causes further disrespect toward you and further disregard of the marriage covenant.

Regardless of his decision, be respectful in the face of his disrespect.

> "It is God's will that you should be sanctified: that you should avoid sexual immorality; that each of you should learn to control your own body in a way that is holy and honorable."
> (1 Thessalonians 4:3–4)

#3 Necessary Separation

QUESTION: "My husband has been seeing prostitutes. Spiritual leaders say that divorce is not an option—that I must continue to submit to my adulterous husband. Must I continue exposing myself to sexual disease? I feel I am setting an example before my children of condoning this behavior."

ANSWER: The advice of your spiritual leaders is not biblically accurate. In Matthew 5:32 and 19:9, Jesus speaks against divorce *"except for sexual immorality."* Divorce is *permitted* (not commanded) in instances of adultery.

One single instance of unfaithfulness followed by a repentant heart is one thing. Risking your health and exposing your children to continuous immorality is another.

▶ Since God's heart for the marriage relationship is reconciliation, if there is a true change in his behavior, your position is to be open and receptive.

▶ Pray for God's leading in your life. At the very least, you certainly are permitted to separate from your husband sexually in order to uphold your God-given responsibility to keep the marital bed pure.

> "Good judgment wins favor,
> but the way of the unfaithful
> leads to their destruction."
> (Proverbs 13:15)

#4 Marriage Bed Honored

QUESTION: "My husband left me for another woman and says he doesn't want to be married anymore. He refuses to get marriage counseling, but when he comes to see the children, he wants to spend the night with me. Should I let him?"

ANSWER: The spouse who leaves his marriage partner, engages in a sexual union with another woman, and refuses marriage counseling should not have marriage privileges. He's wanting you physically outside of marriage, without the emotional bonding inside of marriage. Realize that the marriage bed is part of the marriage covenant, and should be honored by all.

> "Marriage should be honored by all,
> and the marriage bed kept pure,
> for God will judge the adulterer
> and all the sexually immoral."
> (Hebrews 13:4)

#5 Sharing Your Story

QUESTION: "My friends are beginning divorce proceedings as a result of adultery. In the past I committed adultery and subsequently experienced a devastating divorce. Is it appropriate for me to try to talk with the offending party about this decision?"

ANSWER: Extending care and concern for a couple on the brink of divorce could possibly save their marriage. The most effective people to help others gain victory in their lives are those who have struggled with the same temptations and have learned valuable truths through those trials.

▶ When God guides you to share a personal failure, speak the truth in love.

▶ Share the specifics of what you learned the hard way.

In this way, you can be the Lord's instrument to communicate the value of consistency and commitment, and you might save a marriage.

> "A truthful witness saves lives. ... "
> (Proverbs 14:25)

#6 Unexpected Pregnancy

QUESTION: "My husband had an affair with a married woman, and now she is expecting his child. He is willing to help her financially, but she also wants my husband to be involved in the child's life. We feel involvement with the child would be too disruptive to our own family. In this situation, what should we do?"

ANSWER: This complex situation requires a multi-faceted answer:

▶ First, your husband would be wise to confirm his paternity.

▶ If he is the father, then he *must* take full responsibility for his behavior and be financially responsible.

▶ After that, all decisions need to be made in light of what is in the best interest of the child, as well as the children in your family.

▶ With two families connected by adultery, usually the best option for the child is to be raised and nurtured within the security of one family and one alone. Any other arrangement could open the door to deceit, temptation, and discord.

No good purpose is served in telling others, especially if a child can be protected from crude name-calling, which so often surrounds the stigma of being an "illegitimate child." Realize, the child did nothing illegitimate, only the two who were involved in the adulterous affair. At a later time in life, the situation could be different. No matter what decision you make, do not lie to the child or to anyone else.

> "Discretion will protect you,
> and understanding will guard you."
> (Proverbs 2:11)

#7 Unmet Needs

QUESTION: "My wife has not been meeting my needs, and now I've met a wonderful woman who makes me feel like a man. We are drawn to each other. What should I do?"

ANSWER: Any woman who draws a married man away from his wife is not "wonderful." Once she realized she was romantically drawn to you—or you to her—she should have encouraged you to be faithful to your wife and turned away from any romantic involvement with you. Now, you need to turn away from her.

> "Do not let your heart turn to her ways
> or stray into her paths."
> (Proverbs 7:25)

#8 Continuing Contact after an Affair

QUESTION: "After having an illicit affair, I became a Christian and my life truly changed. I've been writing this man in the hope that he will be saved. I want to be true to my commitment to my husband, but how do I overcome the strong emotions I still feel for the other man?"

ANSWER: You made a commitment to remain true to your marriage covenant. Since feelings are merely responders to thinking, don't allow your thoughts to dwell on this other man.

▶ Don't even dwell on his salvation—ultimately, God is the author of salvation.

▶ Stop writing to him about salvation. Your motive probably will be misunderstood, and your husband will continue to be hurt.

▶ Flee your extramarital passion by focusing on being a person of Christlike purity.

"Flee the evil desires of youth and pursue righteousness, faith, love and peace, along with those who call on the Lord out of a pure heart" (2 Timothy 2:22).

▶Trust in your Creator to persevere with endurance.

"Blessed is the one who perseveres under trial because, having stood the test, that person will receive the crown of life that the Lord has promised to those who love him" (James 1:12).

HOW TO Find Peace through Pain

The painful lessons of adultery are taught only too well in the story of King David, the most famous adulterer in history. The fact that David is remembered as a great king and a man after God's own heart (1 Samuel 13:14) shows the completeness of God's mercy after a personal moral failure.

But for those who have become stained by the sin of adultery, for those who are repentant and cry out to God to be restored, *be assured* that you can find the freedom of forgiveness. You can find peace in the midst of pain.

If you enter a season of suffering—whether as a result of your mate's infidelity or your own sexual sin—be assured that God promises to give you peace with His assurance of safety.

"In peace I will lie down and sleep, for you alone, LORD, make me dwell in safety."
(Psalm 4:8)

▶ **Be thankful** for all that God is teaching you.

"Give thanks in all circumstances; for this is God's will for you in Christ Jesus" (1 Thessalonians 5:18).

▶ **Pray** for the heavenly Father to reveal and change your offensive responses.

"If you are offering your gift at the altar and there remember that your brother or sister has something against you, leave your gift there in front of the altar. First go and be reconciled to them; then come and offer your gift" (Matthew 5:23–24).

▶ **Allow** His love to increase your love for the offender.

"My command is this: Love each other as I have loved you" (John 15:12).

▶ **Wait** for the Holy Spirit to break the strongholds that are blocking effective communication.

"The weapons we fight with are not the weapons of the world. On the contrary, they have divine power to demolish strongholds. We demolish arguments and every pretension that sets itself up against the knowledge of God, and we take captive every thought to make it obedient to Christ" (2 Corinthians 10:4–5).

▶**Believe** with faith that all things are possible with the One who created all things.

" ... *all things are possible with God*" (Mark 10:27).

Regaining Trust

QUESTION: "My husband was unfaithful to me last year. Is it possible for me to ever trust him again? Is it possible for him to change?"

ANSWER: It is possible for your husband to regain your trust—but:

▶First he must develop a godly sorrow over his lack of commitment to you and the marriage covenant.

▶Then he needs to identify the key that opened the door to adultery.

▶Through Christian marriage counseling, he must admit and understand his weaknesses and then devise a plan to keep from walking through that door again. Pray that he will see his sin as God sees it and hate his sin as God hates it.

It is possible for God to change anyone who is *willing* to have a changed heart.

"For nothing will be impossible with God."
(Luke 1:37 ESV)

The Myth of Greener Grass

Her fall into sin seems innocent at first: a husband she loves who does his own thing. He's traveling a lot on the job or he's gone off with his buddies—at a game, golf course, or gun show. He's a good provider and father ... when he's home.

She chaperones slumber parties and spends time with friends, especially when the kids are at camp. They have what everyone would call a beautiful life, yet she knows something is missing.

The hole in her heart longs for words of endearment instead of just, "What are we having for dinner?" or "Did you pick up my suit?" After the kids are at school or asleep, she remembers the passion they shared and tries to fill her emptiness with happily-ever-after tales.

There's a man in the office who appreciates her, he values her excellent work. He smiles at her and makes her laugh. He says how nice she looks. Their exchanges seem so innocent, so harmless. Then, when pangs of guilt bubble up, she quickly bursts those emotions, rationalizing, "We're not doing anything wrong!"

She rushes to work early and then stays late, simply because *he is there*. She dresses carefully, as if for a date, holding up outfits before the mirror wondering what *he will think*. Casual lunches along with a crowd become dinners for two late after work. Their time starts lighthearted with laughter, but soon turns serious ... and dangerous.

She waves off every warning, smothers the hint of shame, and ignores the guilt of betrayal. And her justification is classic, "Don't I deserve to be happy?" Headfirst, she falls into what she calls *love*, but in truth, it's really a *lie*. The grass is *not* greener on the other side.

Ensnared in an affair, she shuffles between two worlds. In both she pretends to be someone she's not. She is *not a single woman*, nor is she *a faithful wife*.

Joy escapes her. Peace eludes her. Juggling all the lies she tells and the lies she believes becomes too much to manage. She calls it off again and again. She's ready to quit her job, ready to confess her sin, ready to jump off a bridge because she can no longer face the woman she sees in the mirror. No longer does she see a confident woman, only her shameful secret.

Over time, too many lies lead to inconsistent answers that result in feared confrontation. Tearfully, she confesses the truth to her husband. It's a load off her mind and heart, but it's still a burden to bear and it's agony to witness the pain she's caused. She begs and pleads for his forgiveness. She quits her job and promises it will never happen again. But what can she do with the lingering guilt, the shame that constantly shadows her? Both are constant companions no matter where she tries to hide.

She struggles to believe her husband can forgive and forget. They muddle through the mess she's made and try to put the pieces of their shattered lives back together again. Grateful that he loves her despite her betrayal, she accepts guilt as the penalty for her sin and carries it with her like a shroud of shame.

Although she has confessed the truth to her husband, she is afraid to confess it to before her Lord—even though she's aware that He *already* knows. How can He ever forgive her? How could He love her after what she's done?

Repentant, she brings the burden of her brokenness—her guilt and her shame—to the foot of the cross. She leaves it there, only to run back and pick it up again and again, to punish herself again and again.

Then she reads of Jesus' love and redemption: the woman at the well, the woman who washes Jesus' feet with her tears, and especially the woman caught in adultery. She identifies with each of these broken, but blessed women. Finally, she realizes that by judging herself, she is placing herself above the authority of her God and her King, the One who asked the woman caught in adultery about her accusers, *"Woman, where are they? Has no one condemned you?"* She replies, *"No one, sir,"* and then hears these sweet words from the Lover of her soul, who would sacrifice everything for her: *"Then neither do I condemn you. ... Go now and leave your life of sin"* (John 8:9–11). And she does because she has a Savior, and in Him...

"There is now no condemnation for those who are in Christ Jesus." (Romans 8:1)

Why is adultery so deceptive?
Because it gives the illusion of being
loved—a flawed feeling of connection
and a false sense of security.
So, instead of living in a fantasy world,
live by the truth of God's holy Word,
keeping the marriage covenant pure.

—June Hunt

SCRIPTURES TO MEMORIZE

Can a man have a secret affair and no one get **burned** by it?

> *"Can a man scoop fire into his lap without his clothes being **burned**?"* (Proverbs 6:27)

As a child of **God**, I **belong to Him in body and spirit**. Does being **unfaithful** to my spouse have any effect on my children?

> *"Has not the one **God** made you? You **belong to him in body and spirit**. And what does the one God seek? Godly offspring. So be on your guard, and do not be **unfaithful** to the wife of your youth."* (Malachi 2:15)

Does **sexual immorality** have any adverse effect on my **body**?

> *"Flee from **sexual immorality**. All other sins a person commits are outside the body, but whoever sins sexually, sins against their own **body**."* (1 Corinthians 6:18)

Can a person **be deceived** and **God mocked**, or will an adulterer **reap what he sows**?

> *"Do not **be deceived**: **God** cannot be **mocked**. A man **reaps what he sows**."* (Galatians 6:7)

What consequences occur when a man **sleeps with another man's wife** and **touches her**?

> *"So is he who **sleeps with another man's wife**; no one who **touches her** will go unpunished."* (Proverbs 6:29)

Can a person discretely **commit adultery** and no one be **destroyed** by it?

*"But a man who **commits adultery** has no sense; whoever does so **destroys** himself."* (Proverbs 6:32)

Are **sexual thoughts evil**? If I keep them **inside** and don't act on them, can they still **defile** me?

*"For it is from within, out of a person's heart, that **evil thoughts** come—**sexual** immorality, theft, murder, adultery, greed, malice, deceit, lewdness, envy, slander, arrogance and folly. All these evils come from **inside** and **defile** a person."* (Mark 7:21–23)

Adultery seems commonplace today, even among Christians. **Will God** still **judge the adulterer**?

*"Marriage should be honored by all, and the marriage bed kept pure, for **God will judge the adulterer** and all the sexually immoral."* (Hebrews 13:4)

Will God provide a **way out** when I am **tempted**?

*"No temptation has overtaken you except what is common to mankind. And **God** is faithful; he will not let you be **tempted** beyond what you can bear. ... he **will** also **provide a way** out."* (1 Corinthians 10:13)

Is it **God's will** that I **avoid sexual immorality**?

*"It is **God's will** that you should be sanctified: that you should **avoid sexual immorality**."* (1 Thessalonians 4:3)

NOTES

1. Merriam-Webster, Inc., *Merriam-Webster's Collegiate Dictionary*, Eleventh ed. (Springfield, MA: Merriam-Webster, Inc., 2003), s.v. "Adultery."

2. J. Strong, *Enhanced Strong's Lexicon* (Bellingham, WA: Logos Bible Software, 2001), #H5003.

3. Strong, *Enhanced Strong's Lexicon*, #G4202.

4. Beth Laurence, "Debt and Marriage: When Do I Owe My Spouse's Debts?" (Berkeley, CA: NOLO, 2013), http://www.nolo.com/legal-encyclopedia/debt-marriage-owe-spouse-debts-29572.html.

5. Lawrence J. Crabb, Jr., *Understanding People: Deep Longings for Relationship*, Ministry Resources Library (Grand Rapids: Zondervan, 1987), 15–16; Robert S. McGee, *The Search for Significance*, 2nd ed. (Houston, TX: Rapha, 1990), 27–30.

6. Kay Marshall Strom, *Helping Women in Crisis: A Handbook for People Helpers* (Grand Rapids: Zondervan, 1986), 90-91.

7. Strom, *Helping Women in Crisis*, 93–96.

8. Strom, *Helping Women in Crisis*, 90–91.

9. Strom, *Helping Women in Crisis*, 93–96.

10. Van Cleave, Byrd, and Revell, *Counseling for Substance Abuse and Addiction*, 83–6; Carolyn Johnson, *Understanding Alcoholism* (Grand Rapids: Zondervan, 1991), 145–50; Christina B. Parker, *When Someone You Love Drinks Too Much: A Christian Guide to Addiction, Codependence, & Recovery* (New York: Harper & Row, 1990), 55–56.

11. Van Cleave, Byrd, and Revell, *Counseling for Substance Abuse and Addiction*, 87.

SELECTED BIBLIOGRAPHY

Alcorn, Randy C. *Christians in the Wake of the Sexual Revolution: Recovering Our Sexual Sanity*. A Critical Concern Book. Portland, OR: Multnomah, 1985.

Carder, Dave, and Duncan Jaenicke. *Torn Asunder: Recovering from Extramarital Affairs*. Rev. and expanded ed. Chicago: Moody, 1995.

Carter, Les. *The Prodigal Spouse*. Minirth-Meier Series. Nashville: Thomas Nelson, 1990.

Harley, Willard F., Jr., and Jennifer Harley Chalmers. *Surviving an Affair*. Grand Rapids: Fleming H. Revell, 1998.

Hunt, June. *Counseling Through Your Bible Handbook*. Eugene, Oregon: Harvest House Publishers, 2008.

Hunt, June. *Hope for Your Heart: Finding Strength in Life's Storms*. Wheaton, IL: Crossway, 2011.

Hunt, June. *How to Deal with Difficult Relationships: Bridging the Gaps that Separate People*. Eugene, OR: Harvest House, 2012.

Hunt, June. *How to Defeat Harmful Habits: Freedom from Six Addictive Behaviors*. Eugene, OR: Harvest House, 2011.

Hunt, June. *How to Forgive . . . When You Don't Feel Like It*. Eugene, OR: Harvest House Publishers, 2007.

Hunt, June. *How to Handle Your Emotions*. Eugene, OR: Harvest House Publishers, 2008.

Hunt, June. *Seeing Yourself Through God's Eyes*. Eugene, OR: Harvest House Publishers, 2008.

Lutzer, Erwin W. *Living with Your Passions*. Wheaton, IL: Victor, 1983.

Mylander, Charles. *Running the Red Lights: Putting the Brakes on Sexual Temptation*. Regal: Ventura, CA, 1986.

Neal, Connie. *Holding on to Heaven While Your Friend Goes Through Hell*. Nashville: Word, 1999.

Peterson, J. Allan. *The Myth of the Greener Grass*. Wheaton, IL: Tyndale House, 1983.

Rainey, Dennis. *Lonely Husbands, Lonely Wives: Rekindling Intimacy in Every Marriage*. Dallas: Word, 1989.

Strom, Kay Marshall. *Helping Women in Crisis: A Handbook for People Helpers*. Grand Rapids: Zondervan, 1986.

Virkler, Henry A. *Broken Promises*. Contemporary Christian Counseling, ed. Gary R. Collins. Dallas: Word, 1992.

West, Kari. *Dare to Trust Dare to Hope Again: Living with Losses of the Heart*. Colorado Springs, CO: Faithful Woman, 2002.

Winebrenner, Jan, and Debra Frazier. *When a Leader Falls What Happens to Everyone Else?* Minneapolis, MN: Bethany, 1993.

June Hunt's HOPE FOR THE HEART booklets are biblically-based, and full of practical advice that is relevant, spiritually-fulfilling and wholesome. Each topic presents scriptural truths and examples of real-life situations to help readers relate and integrate June's counseling guidance into their own lives. Practical for individuals from all walks of life, this new booklet series invites readers into invaluable restoration, emotional health, and spiritual freedom. Available in a display for churches and ministries.

HOPE FOR THE HEART TITLES

www.aspirepress.com